TO

JOSHUA

LOVE FROM

Uncle James & Auntie Michelle

xx

Joshua has a pet unlike any other. He doesn't have whiskers, or fur, or cute fluffy ears.

He doesn't fetch sticks in the park, or chase his tail, and he can't curl up in Joshua's lap for a snooze.

But he does have three LITTLE toes.

And a L-O-N-G neck.

And an even L-O-N-G-E-R tail.

And that's because Joshua's pet is a dinosaur.

Called Dexter.

Although Dexter can't meow, or bark, or squeak, or moo, or quack, he does have a great big roar. Just not today.

"It's ... gone," whispered Dexter. "Yesterday I was roaring loads, but now there's nothing. Not even a growl."

"It can't have vanished completely," said Joshua. "We'll just have to look for it. Come on, let's go!"

And so their great roar hunt began....

First, Joshua and Dexter searched the park. As they walked around, Joshua thought he could hear something. Could it really be Dexter's roar?

OOMPAH! OOMPAH! OOMPAH!

"That's not my roar, that's a brass band!" said Dexter.

"Carry on walking down the road," said the band leader. "I'm sure I heard something earlier today that could have been a roar."

"Thanks!" said Joshua. "Let's go, Dexter!"

TOOOOT
POM
POM
POM

Suddenly, Joshua and Dexter heard a booming sound that got louder and louder.

But the closer and closer they got, the less and less it sounded like a roar.

BOOM! BOOM! BOOM!

Joshua turned to Dexter: "That's not ..."

"... my roar," frowned Dexter.

"Ha! My wrecking ball's never been mistaken for a dinosaur roar before," chuckled the crane driver. "Try the beach, there's always strange noises coming from there."

"Phew," said Joshua. "All this roar hunting is tiring work. Come on, let's get an ice cream."

As Joshua and Dexter wandered across the sand they heard a distant sound getting closer.

"Uh-oh, what's that?" said Dexter.

SQUAWK! SQUAWK! SQUAWK!

"Aaahh! Seagulls!" shouted Joshua. "They're after the ice cream! Time for more roar hunting!"

FIRE

They ran and ran and ran until they could run no more.

Suddenly, Dexter spotted something big, red and shiny coming towards them. It was their friendly neighbourhood firefighters.

"Hey, our siren can make a noise as big as a roar," they said. "Will that do?"

NEE-NAW! NEE-NAW! NEE-NAW!

"Hmm, it's kind of close, but it's still not really a roar," said Joshua.

"It's a nee-no from me," said Dexter.

"Why don't you try asking a vet why your roar's disappeared?" said the firefighters. "We'll take you to see our friend – hop in!"

"I've never ever examined a dinosaur before," said the vet. "Oh well, here goes!"

"AAAHHH," said Dexter as she looked down his throat.

"EEEEK," said Dexter as she looked in his ears.

"WAA, that tickles," said Dexter as she examined his tummy.

"Well, this is strange, I can't see anything," puzzled the vet. "Why don't you go to the school library and hunt for your roar there?"

DOG
CAT

BRRRRIIINNGGG
SCHOOL

Joshua spotted his best friend's brother in the playground.

"Dinosaur books?" he said. "Yes, there's loads in the library. Go in the main door and just follow the signs."

"Come on, Dexter, let's go!" said Joshua.

"WHAT?" shouted Dexter.

"The library!" explained Joshua.

"WHAT?!" yelled Dexter.

"Unblock your ears, Dexter!" said Joshua.

"WHAT?!?" bellowed Dexter.

And so the great roar hunt continued as they tiptoed into the library, trying their best not to be heard.

Joshua glanced back. "Whatever you do, Dexter, don't ..." *CLONK!* "... hit your head on the light shade. Or ..."

THUMP! THUMP! THUMP!

"... knock any books off the shelves. Or ..." *SSHHHH!* "... upset the librarian."

Joshua sighed. "Are you sure you're not a clumsy-saurus?!"

SHHH!
A
QUIET PLEASE
DICTIONARY
MAPS OF THE WORLD

D
E

They quickly found a comfy spot and started flicking through the dinosaur books.

"Any luck?" asked Joshua.

"Not yet," replied Dexter. "Oh wait, look!"

Joshua peeked round excitedly.

"I think that's a picture of my Uncle Dave in this one!" chuckled Dexter.

Book after book, page after page, they hunted and hunted until Joshua noticed a big blue book tucked away in the corner.

"Hang on, that one's wobbling," said Joshua.

"What. Is. That?" said Dexter.

Joshua took a deep breath and opened it up. A ginormous roar erupted from the pages and whooshed into Dexter's mouth.

"RRRROOOOOAAAAAARRRR!"

"YAAAAYYYY!" cheered Joshua.

"SHHHHHHH!" hissed the librarian.

"ROAR," whispered Dexter happily.

RRRRROOOAARRRR!

After a long day of brass band listening, seagull dodging, fire engine riding, puppy playing, library tiptoeing, head clonking and roar finding, Joshua and Dexter headed back home.

"What a roar-some day!" they cheered.

"Yay for roars and dino-snores," thought Joshua as he drifted off to sleep and began to dream of his next BIG adventure....

GO DIVING?
Maybe I'll...

MEET SANTA?

EXPLORE SPACE?

Joshua, look out for more **Mini Adventures** books.
Go to www.orangutanbooks.co.uk

Story by M.K. Scott
Illustrated by Jo Lindley
Designed by Ryan Dunn

orangutan

First published by Orangutan Books in 2019
Hometown World Ltd, 1 Queen Street, Bath BA1 1HE

Visit
www.orangutanbooks.co.uk
Follow us @orangutanbooks

ISBN 978-1-78979-543-1

Printed in Italy
HTW_PO201929

FSC
www.fsc.org
MIX
Paper from responsible sources
FSC® C023419

Level 2 - Red

BookLife

Helpful Hints for Reading at Home

The graphemes (written letters) and phonemes (units of sound) used throughout this series are aligned with Letters and Sounds. This offers a consistent approach to learning whether reading at home or in the classroom.

HERE IS A LIST OF PHONEMES FOR THIS PHASE OF LEARNING. AN EXAMPLE OF THE PRONUNCIATION CAN BE FOUND IN BRACKETS.

Phase 2			
s (sat)	a (cat)	t (tap)	p (tap)
i (pin)	n (net)	m (man)	d (dog)
g (go)	o (sock)	c (cat)	k (kin)
ck (sack)	e (elf)	u (up)	r (rabbit)
h (hut)	b (ball)	f (fish)	ff (off)
l (lip)	ll (ball)	ss (hiss)	

HERE ARE SOME WORDS WHICH YOUR CHILD MAY FIND TRICKY.

Phase 2 Tricky Words			
the	to	I	no
go	into		

TOP TIPS FOR HELPING YOUR CHILD TO READ:

- Allow children time to break down unfamiliar words into units of sound and then encourage children to string these sounds together to create the word.
- Encourage your child to point out any focus phonics when they are used.
- Read through the book more than once to grow confidence.
- Ask simple questions about the text to assess understanding.
- Encourage children to use illustrations as prompts.

PHASE 2

/ss/

This book focuses on the phoneme /ss/ and is a red level 2 book band.

Can you say this sound and draw it with your finger?

It is Ness. Ness is a pet.

Ness can hop a lot!

It is Bess. Bess is fun.

Bess can hiss a lot!

It is Tim. Tim is a cat.

Tim can get a lot of fuss.

It is Kim. Kim is a dog.

No! It is a big mess!

BookLife Publishing

BookLife Readers

King's Lynn, Norfolk PE30 4LS

ISBN 978-1-83927-897-6

A catalogue record for this book is available from the British Library.

Pets
Written by William Anthony
Designed by Jasmine Pointer

An Introduction to BookLife Readers...

Our Readers have been specifically created in line with the London Institute of Education's approach to book banding and are phonetically decodable and ordered to support each phase of the Letters and Sounds document.

Each book has been created to provide the best possible reading and learning experience. Our aim is to share our love of books with children, providing both emerging readers and prolific page-turners with beautiful books that are guaranteed to provoke interest and learning, regardless of ability.

BOOK BAND GRADED using the Institute of Education's approach to levelling.

PHONETICALLY DECODABLE supporting each phase of Letters and Sounds.

EXERCISES AND QUESTIONS to offer reinforcement and to ascertain comprehension.

CLEAR DESIGN to inspire and provoke engagement, providing the reader with clear visual representations of each non-fiction topic.

AUTHOR INSIGHT:
WILLIAM ANTHONY

Despite his young age, William Anthony's involvement with children's education is quite extensive. He has written over 60 titles with BookLife Publishing so far, across a wide range of subjects. William graduated from Cardiff University with a 1st Class BA (Hons) in Journalism, Media and Culture, creating an app and a TV series, among other things, during his time there.

William Anthony has also produced work for the Prince's Trust, a charity created by HRH The Prince of Wales, that helps young people with their professional future. He has created animated videos for a children's education company that works closely with the charity.

PHASE 2
/ss/

This book focuses on the phoneme /ss/ and is a red level 2 book band.

Image Credits Images are courtesy of Shutterstock.com. With thanks to Getty Images, Thinkstock Photo and iStockphoto. Cover – Eric Isselee, PetlinDmitry, mangpor2004, effective stock photos. 4 – Victoria Paladiy. 5 – anetapics. 6–7 – Sergey Novikov. 8 – uzhursky. 9 – Namning. 10 – Marina Fistina. 11 – Ksenia Raykova.

BookLife Non-Fiction
Readers
EXPLORE A WORLD OF NON-FICTION WITH OUR DECODABLE READER RANGE
Caterpillar to Butterfly
9781839278938
Chinese New Year
9781839278921
Dig a Pit
9781839278945
Tap the Puck
9781839278952
Pets
9781839278976
Picnic
9781839278969
Queens and Kings
9781839278990
Vets
9781839278983
At the Fun Fair
9781839279010
Look Up!
9781839279003
At the Shop
9781839279027
The Fixer's Lesson on: Screws
9781839279034
Stay Safe Online
9781839279058
Habitats
9781839279041
A woodland is a habitat too. Woodlands have a lot of trees. Trees can have birds living in them. Some birds can sing a tune!
MORE COMING SOON
BookLife PUBLISHING

Lexile and AR levelled
CERTIFIED LEXILE PARTNER
L&S
BASED ON LETTERS & SOUNDS
PHONETICALLY DECODABLE
Readers
The Little Painter
By Shalini Vallepur
Readers
Flynn's Fantastic Flight
By A H Benjamin
Readers
The Smell that Wasn't Funny
FREE ONLINE RESOURCES AVAILABLE
Readers
The Monster Cook Book
Readers
The Human Under My Bed and King for the Day
Illustrated By Irene Renon
Readers
Mummy's Tummy
BOOK-BANDED FICTION FROM LILAC TO LIME
FREE DOWNLOADABLE RESOURCES FOR EACH TITLE AVAILABLE ONLINE
Accelerated Reader

BookLife Readers

The BookLife Readers begin with the very basics of phonetically decodable reading. Starting with the earliest step of CVC words – words comprising a consonant, a vowel and a consonant – and building on this combination slowly, the reader follows a prescribed format taken directly from the recognised Letters and Sounds educational document.

By aligning our books with Letters and Sounds, we offer our readers a consistent approach to learning, whether at home or in the classroom. Books levelled as 'a' are an introduction to the band. Readers can advance to 'b' where graphemes are consolidated and further graphemes are introduced. The illustrations guide the reader, helping to deliver reading progression through the scheme in a **colourful** and **exciting** way. As a reader moves through the book band levels, the page numbers, level of repetition and sentence structure complexity all advance at a rate which **encourages development** without halting enjoyment.

To find out more about this exciting new reading scheme, visit www.booklife.co.uk

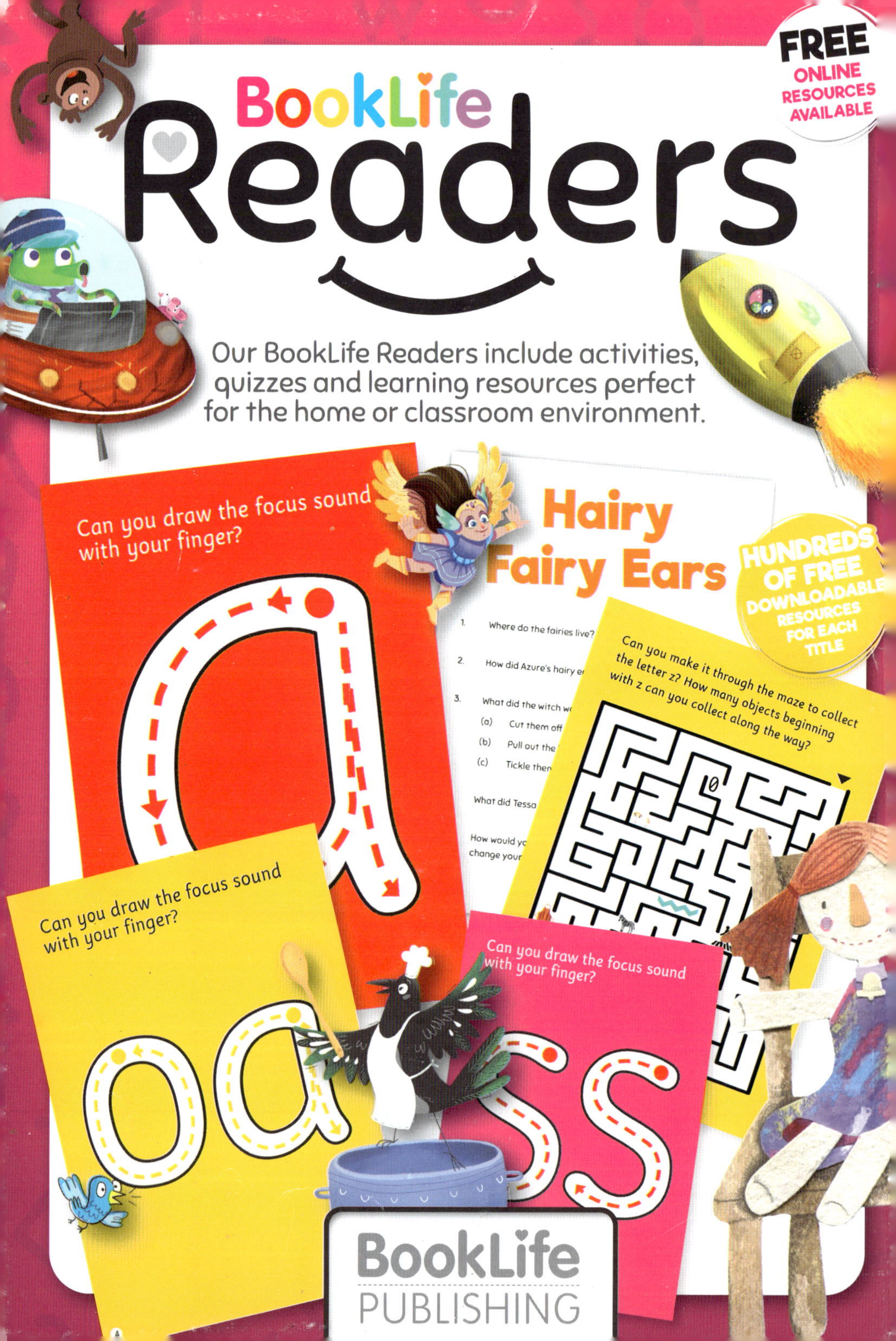
BookLife
Readers
FREE
ONLINE
RESOURCES
AVAILABLE
Our BookLife Readers include activities, quizzes and learning resources perfect for the home or classroom environment.
Can you draw the focus sound with your finger?
Hairy Fairy Ears
1. Where do the fairies live?
2. How did Azure's hairy e
3. What did the witch w
(a) Cut them off
(b) Pull out the
(c) Tickle then
What did Tessa
How would yo
change your
HUNDREDS OF FREE DOWNLOADABLE RESOURCES FOR EACH TITLE
Can you make it through the maze to collect the letter z? How many objects beginning with z can you collect along the way?
Can you draw the focus sound with your finger?
Can you draw the focus sound with your finger?
BookLife
PUBLISHING